Contents

Introduction

1 - Is The Handyman Business For You?

2 - Inventory of Your Tools

3 - Home Repair Vehicle and Space

4 - Licensing, Accounting, and Taxes

5 - Licensing, Accounting, and Taxes

6 - Getting Started

7 - Using Your Computer and The Internet

8 - How Much To Charge and Why

9- Contracting Jobs

10 - Getting Help

11 - Safety

12 - Final

Glossary

Introduction

In 2009, the economy was in crisis and thousands of jobs were being lost every day. The national unemployment rate had reached nine percent, and some areas had seen it rise to twelve percent. The Covid-19 pandemic in 2020 has brought about even more problems for many. Although the financial markets appear to have survived the worst, many employees are still suffering from high unemployment. Those who can work remotely are more likely to be in the majority of the affected fields.

Even after the initial stimulus package, the unemployment compensation programs were oversubscribed with applications for assistance exceeding records. Many people reached the end of their eligibility and were still unable workable.

Many people took drastic pay cuts, but they were happy to have enough money to pay their bills and keep them afloat. Many people with jobs lost their homes due to their inability to pay their mortgages. It remains a grim picture for many Americans.

These individuals often have handyman (home repair) skills that they could use to quickly increase their income with minimal investment. Home improvement and repair was and is still a multi-billion-dollar business. Home Depots, Lowes and other stores that sell home improvements across the country reflect the popularity of home repairs.

As I type this revision, it seems that the pandemic is growing and it's hard to see where it will end. To avoid Covid, people are staying put and aren't considering buying larger homes. This creates a huge market for home-owners and those with skills in home improvement and repair. Major remodeling is often the work of professional home contractors. Many of the smaller jobs can be a source of income for people with basic skills in home repairs.

The average hourly rate of a self-employed handyman is $60 to $75 at the time this book was written. This is a significant increase from when it was first published. Despite the fact that wages are still low, home repairs pay more and can be done by those who have additional skills.

Every homeowner is constantly making improvements and repairs to their home. Many homeowners will require some assistance at one point or another.

This book is a sign of your desire to help these thousands of homeowners and business owners across America get their repairs done right and at a reasonable price.

Handyman business and home repair business can be interchanged in this book. Both names can be used to refer to the same business. Handyman is a term that describes a person who does various repairs to a house or office. It could be a woman or a man. Anyone can use this book to make some extra money and start a small, financially successful business.

You already have the skills to start a business if you've been doing repairs on your own house or helping friends and family with their home repairs. This book will help expand your skills and turn them into a profit-making business.

There are franchise opportunities for handyman businesses. You can search for handyman to see it all. While joining a franchise is a great way to start, you can also do it yourself and make more profit using the information in this guide. You can also manage your activities and keep pricing competitive. Chapter 1 discusses the first step, which is to decide if the business is right for you.

It is important to take a detailed inventory of your skills once you have decided that a home-based business is right for you. Different people have different skills, and each person has different levels. You need to identify your strengths and areas that you can improve. This will help you make the most of your work and maximize profit. Chapter 2 helps you identify your strengths and how to help others.

Tools and Work Vehicle

While home repair calls for a good collection of tools, it is not essential to have more expensive tools in order to get the job done. Most home repairs can be done with the tools you already have.

Chapter Three will show you how to make the most of the tools that you have, and how to use the consumer-level tools that you do need to purchase. Chapter 4 will help you set up a work vehicle that can be used for any job.

Accounting, Licensing and Taxes

Once you have completed your inventories and feel ready to start the business, you need to decide on all the licensing, accounting and tax issues. It will vary depending on where you live and what level of work you do. This will not be the case for someone doing part-time work or someone working full-time. It is important to have all this in place before you contact a customer. Chapter Five will help you ensure that your business complies with all community requirements. It also explains how to ensure your business meets all tax codes of the Internal Revenue Service.

Getting Started

Now it is time to get started on the most important step, making your business visible to as many people possible. Businesses need customers to succeed. Chapter Six provides basic, low-cost marketing and advertising techniques that can quickly bring in customers. It also addresses the crucial topic of maintaining customers. Although it is vital for any business to attract new customers, it is much more expensive to retain the customers you already have. The potential of email and social media has made this chapter much more interesting since 2009.

Use Your Computer and the Internet

Computers can be used to manage many aspects of small businesses, including accounting, marketing, tax preparation, research, and even accounting. Chapter Seven provides valuable information on how to use your computer as well as a list of great free software that can be used to run your business efficiently.

What is the Charge?

The most complex and important topic in any business is
How much you should charge. This is crucial because too high charges can lead to job losses and low charges will result in you losing money. Your business will be affected in either case. Chapter Eight will provide a clear method for determining the price of your services. It also includes a solid secondary method that can be used

to check your prices after you have calculated them. This chapter will help you decide when to increase your prices in order to get the best possible price for your work.

Contracting Jobs

You may be able to complete some jobs in one to three hours. A verbal agreement between both parties is sufficient. This is true even for jobs that don't require you to purchase materials. Others jobs may require more time and will take longer and require you to purchase additional materials. These jobs will require a contract, drawings and specifications.

It is important to know how much you are paid, but it is even more important to get paid for all your work. It is important to know when a contract is required and how to prepare one. Solid collection procedures are also important. Chapter Nine explains exactly how to collect every job. This book provides clear and concise instructions. It also contains all the forms necessary to run your business. You won't need to spend your time creating them. This chapter contains a link to a website that has a collection of pre-made forms. You can simply change your business name by clicking the link.

Get Help

This book is entirely based on my own experience over many years of running a one-person business. Avoid the hassles and costs of managing employees and payroll. There may be occasions when you need help with a particular job. Chapter Ten explains how to find help without having to hire full-time employees. It also outlines the steps you can take to avoid violating IRS regulations, running into payroll deductions or Social Security issues.

Your skills

This book assumes you have sufficient home repair skills to perform various types of repairs in return for fair compensation. There is always more to learn, no matter what your level of skill.

To improve the quality of your work, keep an open mind and be willing to learn new things.

Safety

Chapter Eleven is the most important chapter in this book. It is all about safety. If used with care or lack of attention, power tools can cause serious injury.

This chapter will provide information that can help you avoid serious injuries that could ruin your business or your entire life.

Final Notes

The final note in Chapter Twelve is a list of tips and tricks that I think you will find useful for running a profitable home repair business.

Notes about personal experiences are included in all chapters. These notes can be very helpful. These notes are clearly marked by indenting and italics.

1 - Is the Handyman Business Right for You?

This question can only be answered honestly by you. Do you feel confident around the house? Are you able to do basic repairs on your own? Are you happy to do these tasks or are you frustrated by the necessity? Before you decide to start a home-repair business, it is important to answer these questions.

It is also important to consider whether this is a good time for a home-based business. The economy is in decline and the job market remains poor, with Covid still hanging over. This is a great time to be handyman. This is a great time to be a handyman.

Are you looking for self-employment?

A home repair business is considered self-employment. All other small businesses should be considered. Your ability to work independently is key to financial success. Self-starting is best. You don't need a boss to supervise your activities or make sure they are done correctly. You are the owner, manager and accountant of a single-person business. You are the only person responsible for all aspects of the business. Your spouse, husband, friend, or relative may help with some work.

Your income can come in spurts, depending on how many jobs you accept. Also, your earnings may fluctuate depending on the amount

of work that is completed. The payment may be delayed if the weather or other problems delay the work. Everything stops, even the income, if you are too sick or injured to work. Everything stops working if you go on vacation or take a day off. You must cover the entire cost of health insurance. The Affordable Health Care Act is not a good option.

There are still ways to make money, even with these issues. Many jobs can be completed in hours, while others may only take a few minutes.

You have the skillset and willingness to apply for the jobs that you are interested in.

They are to be used. Customers may need you to perform the work as they don't have enough skills or are too busy. Others might have the time and skills, but want someone to do the hard work. You may be hired by them for small tasks they can handle. It is important that they hire you for the job. They will also recommend you to other people if you do the job well.

Your customers are your only contact. You should expect to receive calls at odd hours if you have a long job. Customers will call you with complaints. These problems can be difficult to solve without patience and understanding.

Time is money, so it is important to be organized whether you are dealing with problems or a job. You will not only be responsible for existing jobs, but you will also be contacted by people looking for new opportunities. To handle sales calls, you will need to take time off from your current job. Before you can return to the project you were assigned, you will need to work out the price and negotiate with the customer. It is a lot of work, and you must do it all.

This includes not only the home repairs but all related business activities. You are the sole person responsible for all aspects of a business, regardless of who assists you.

This gives you a clear picture of how it is possible to start your own handyman business. Before you jump into any type of business, it is important to understand all the details.

2 - Take a inventory of your tools

Depending on what type of job you are accepting, the tools that you will need for home repair work vary. To be able to take on a wide range of jobs, you will need a good selection of tools. Make a list of all the tools that you have. You may have enough tools if you've been working around your home.

Let's assume that you will be performing basic home repairs such as door repairs, cabinet repairs, or replacement of rotted board. This assumption is only a guideline. You may do other or entirely different tasks. You may need to use different tools in these cases. You don't need to know everything, but you should have a good idea of the tools you will need.

It is important to have all of the tools necessary for the jobs you are contracted to do. The inventory will help you determine if you have all the tools necessary for a job, or if you need to purchase them. Pricing jobs should take into account the cost of such purchases.

This chapter contains a comprehensive list of handyman equipment to help you get started.

What tools do you need to get started?

Below are three lists of useful tools. This first list contains basic hand tools to get you started. The next section contains a list power tools that can be used for many tasks. To save time and increase profits, power tools can make almost all jobs faster. This third list contains additional tools that are helpful, but not essential for getting started.

Start with the basics

Y **Hammers** - You should have a few hammers such as a couple claw hammers, small sledgehammers and a ballpeen hammer

Y **Screwdrivers** - You never know which size or type of screwdriver is needed for what job. I recommend purchasing a complete set that includes phillips, square and torx.

Y **Chisels** - To do doorwork, you'll need chisels. However, a small selection of four sizes is sufficient, including 1/4 inch, 1/2 inches, 3/4 inch and 1 inch.

Should be enough.
Y **Pry Bars** - Also known by Crow Bars, these are useful when you need to remove something from a structure. You can use a large Crow Bar or a smaller flat pry bar.
Y **Nail Set** - Available in three sizes, these are handy for setting new nails or repairing existing ones.
Y **Awl** - Two of these are a good idea as they are easy to lose. This is a great tool for many repairs.
Y **Handsaw** - A good handsaw is essential for certain tasks.
Y **Hacksaw** - For times when metal cutting is required.
Y **Copingsaw** - Small fine cuts may be required in certain repair jobs.
Y **Mallets** - These mallets can be used to protect surfaces from damage caused by a hammer.
Y **Pliers** - Pliers of various sizes and shapes, including a needle nose.
Y **Block plane** - These small planes can be used to smooth out edges and soften corners.
Y **Jack Plane** - To smoothen larger surfaces, such as doors edges. Y **Knives** Several utility knives that have additional blades.
Y **Wrenches** Several sizes, including pipe wrenches and crescent wrenches.
Y **Levels** - Small and large levels. One that is at least 4 feet in length. Y **Squares** - A framing and adjustable square.
Y **Tin Snips** - At least one pair
Y **Coldchisels** - Great for cutting cement. Y **Bolt Cutter** - This tool can be very useful for some jobs.
Y **Tape Measures** - One measuring 12 to 16 feet, and one measuring at least 30 feet for larger areas.
Y **Hatchet** - A small hatchet is handy for some jobs. Y **Caulking Gun** - Used to seal around windows and other surfaces. Y **Staplers** - Handy tool for small repairs
Y **Brushes** - To do some touchup painting. Y **Clamps** - These clamps can be used to secure things as needed.

Y **Saw Horses** - To make your life easier. These plastic folding units are ideal for this purpose because they can be easily carried in your car.

Although this is a comprehensive list, there are likely to be other items that you would like.

You may need to buy for certain jobs, so you should always have extra money for unexpected purchases.

This next list contains power tools that are essential for home repairs. Some tools may not be necessary for your job so wait until you need them.

Power Tools

Y **Drill bits** - This tool is essential for all home repairs. A good drill is essential, as well as a variety of bits, including bits for concrete, wood, and metal.

Y **Circular saw** - This tool is essential for many home repairs. Accessories such as a rip fence attachment or various carbide-tipped knives are also recommended.

Y **Router, and router bits** - This tool can be used for many purposes including creating decorative edges. A small number of carbide-tipped bits is also needed.

Y **Belt Sander** - This is an important tool for rough sanding surfaces. You will need several sanding wheels of different grits and 100-grit.

The Y **Random Orbit sander** is an excellent tool that allows for quick sanding and leaves no swirl marks. You will need several sanding discs with different grits.

Y **Finishing sander** - This handy machine is ideal for fine sanding surfaces. Save time by purchasing specialized sandpaper packets instead of buying full sheets of sandpaper that you need to cut into four pieces.

Y **Sabersaw** - Also known as a jigsaw or a jigsaw it is useful for cutting different shapes. A good selection of blades is available for metal, wood, and plastic.

Y **Spiral Cutting Saw** - Sometimes referred to simply as a zipsaw. This bit can be used to cut irregular shapes on many surfaces. It is similar in shape to a drill bit. You can buy a whole collection.

The Y **Cordless Drill** is as versatile as a regular drill, but it also doubles as a power drill. A bit holder is also available.

Y **Electric Planer** - This is an indispensable tool for anyone who will be

doing door work.

Y **Electric Cords** - You can have several length cords to ensure you are able to use the right one for the job and avoid falling over too long cords.

A small compressor that includes one or more pneumatic nailers/staplers may be useful depending on what kind of work you do.

Your home repair vehicle should contain more than the tools mentioned above.

You can choose from a variety of grits for sandpaper, sanding strips, and sanding belts. YA can Mineral Spirits, also known as Paint Thinner.

A YA can of Lacquer Thinner

A YA collection with different sizes of nails.

A good selection of different sizes and types of screws. YTool Boxes are great for carrying tools to the jobsite.

YDuct Tape

Purchasing Power Tools

Many of the tools that you require can be found at your local hardware store. Find companies that specialize in selling tools to tradespeople. If your budget is available, this is the best place for tools to be purchased. Don't forget about the many online shops that sell tools of every kind. Online shopping can help you save money on tools.

Professional handymen will find trade-level tools the most useful, but they are not worth the cost of consumer tools. These tools can be used until your business is profitable. They will save you money and serve you well.

When you're ready to buy tools for trade, you can check out the products in your local shops and then go online to check for special pricing on the models you desire. Be sure to consider shipping costs.

Carbide-Tipped Blades & Bits

Quality carbide-tipped bits and blades are essential for any tool, trade or consumer. Although most power saws have carbide-tipped blades, these are often very inexpensive blades that only have a few teeth. A high-quality blade must have at least 40 teeth.

Sixty teeth in these cases. This will allow you to make a better cut and improve the quality of your work. Carbide-tipped edges are the best choice, whether you're looking for router bits or power saw blades.

Carbide-tipped bits and blades don't need to be sharpened often but they will eventually. This can be done by a professional company. Without the right tools, it is not possible to sharpen carbide edges well. This requires additional tools and lots of time. It is probably better to hire someone to do this job.

Make sure all of your bits and blades are sharpened and ready for use. This will help you do quality work and prevent delays.

3 - Home Repair Vehicle & Space

You can be prepared for any home repairs with either a fully equipped pickup truck or a trailer. You can also use this to transport any material needed to the job site. You will need to make sure that you have enough space to store your tools and keep them easy to find. This will save you time searching for the right tools for each job.

I didn't own a pickup truck or a customer list when I started my business. I began by accepting any home repair job that I could find, no matter how small. I bought an old trailer with low sides that looked like a rental trailer from years ago to do this work. It had a large interior and I made a waterproof cover.

To organize my small projects, I made dividers inside the trailer. As I moved from home repair to woodworking and furniture-making, this old trailer was my best friend for nearly ten years.

I rented a small storage unit and kept the trailer locked in there every night to avoid it being left in front of my house. Every day, I would drive the trailer to my first job and pick it up at 5 a.m. This cost can be avoided if you have enough space in your garage. You should not leave tools in a trailer or truck parked in your driveway. It is safer to store your tools in a locked space than it is to be seen.

A Better Setup

I moved from my trailer to a small pickup truck equipped with a commercial aluminum camper shell. It had doors on both sides that made it easy to access my tools. This setup was much better and I organized my truck's back with wooden boxes that open to the top. These wooden boxes allowed me to have all the tools and supplies I needed for any job. This setup is ideal for handymen.

Aluminum campers also came with racks that could be used to transport materials too large to fit into the truck's bed.

Large vans are often used by home repair professionals because they have large storage spaces for tools and shelves. You can easily walk into the van.

To store your tools, you will need shelves and boxes either side. This has the disadvantage of higher fuel and maintenance expenses. A small pickup truck with an efficient engine would be a better choice to get you started, while still keeping your costs low.

It doesn't matter if you have a truck, a pickup, or a trailer. The important thing is to organize your tools and other supplies so that you don't waste time looking for them. You will be able to do many small jobs in a single day, and this will increase your profits. You will also be less profitable if you waste time searching for the right tools and supplies.

Your Own Garage Space

A garage or other storage space could prove useful in certain home repairs where some of the work can already be done ahead. This is not a requirement and most jobs can be done on-site.

A shop is a great option if you are looking to move on to more difficult work such as building cabinets. You can also use your garage to save money. You should also consider the local regulations and deed restrictions for your subdivision. Because of the noise potential, it is not recommended to have a small shop. These issues are less likely to occur if you live in rural areas.

4-Licensing, Accounting and Taxes

Businesses need to be either home-based or commercial. The requirements vary from one area to the next. Before opening a business, it is important to understand the requirements in your locality. You may be surprised at the differences between communities. This could cause problems.

My business was located in Tampa, Florida. I had to obtain an occupational license. This requirement was not present in Austin. To collect the sales tax in Florida, I needed a sales tax certificate. While one community may have a different licensing requirement, both States require a certificate to collect sales tax. I discovered that the Tangible tax, which is basically an annual tax on equipment used in your business, was collected by both the States. You pay not only a sales tax when your equipment is purchased, but also an annual tax on its value.

Research any taxes and licensing fees that your State and community charges businesses for operating within their borders. You will be able to save time and avoid any fines for not adhering to local laws. It is possible to operate entirely under radar in certain areas and not pay taxes or obtain licenses. However, I do not recommend this. Follow local regulations instead. Participating in the business community is better than not purchasing licenses or registering to run your business. This shows professionalism to potential customers. It will also help you to advertise your business and make your name known to the taxing agencies in your area.

The Internal Revenue Service

Many of us have paid income taxes to IRS for many years. Your income tax preparations will be easy if you work for an employer of reasonable size. The employer deducts taxes from your income, and you receive an annual form detailing how much income was deducted.

Social security and taxes. This removes many of the costs and complications involved in preparing your annual income tax returns, even if they are filed by an income tax preparation firm.

Keep track of all deductions

You must keep track of all costs when you start your business. This will allow you to deduct them from your income. You could face serious financial problems if you don't keep accurate records of your income and expenses. Quickbooks is a popular accounting software that many businesses use. It is a great software. It is important to keep your accounting system up-to-date. It is silly and frustrating to fall behind, then play catch-up later. You will spend hours trying and preparing reports for your business.

Online accounting is a good option if you are a sole proprietor. GoDaddy Online Accounting is what I use and have been using it for many years. This online service is affordable, reliable, convenient, accurate, and secure.

It is essential to have separate accounts for personal and business purposes in order to use GoDaddy Online Accounting. A business checking account is required, as well as a credit card that is used only for business purposes. To accept credit card payments, you will also need a Credit Card Merchant account. I recommend setting up credit card processing through PayPal after many years of using them. It is also possible to open a business savings account.

After you have set up all these accounts, you can sign up to GoDaddy Online Accounting. They will guide you through connecting your accounts to their service. Once completed, they scan all accounts daily and keep track all income and expenses. Although the service can identify where each item should go, it is not perfect. You will need to verify that everything is correct before you sign up. Once everything is correctly identified, the service will automatically handle it. You can get reports from them at any time to manage income taxes, sales taxes, profit and loss statements, among other things.

You may be able to rely on a friend or family member to help you with these tasks. Make sure that you have all the necessary records. You are kept up to date and receive reports at least monthly on the state of your accounts. You, as the owner of the company, should always be aware of your financial position.

Part-time businesses can use a checking account for accounting

You can save money and time if you plan to only run your handyman business part-time. This can be done by opening a separate checking account for business purposes. It is a bad idea to mix business income and expenses with personal funds.

After you open your checking account, ensure that all income earned by your business is deposited to your checking account. You can use a debit or check card to pay all your business bills. It is simple to keep track of your monthly statements if all your income and expenses are managed from one account. You can also sign up online for banking to view and print all of your account information at any time.

When you get your monthly statement, reconcile it and identify the purpose for each expense. You could also create a numbering system to assign each type of expense a number. Advertising is one example.

= 1, Auto Expenses = 2, Repairs = 3, etc. You can then simply place the correct amount next to each expense and keep the statements in a folder to use at the end to calculate your taxes.

You can sign up for paperless banking to print only the portion of your monthly statement you require. This will help reduce the paper you have to keep, as banks often send extra paper and advertisements along with their statements.

Keep your records clear and concise

Whatever method you use for accounting, it is important to keep it current and keep receipts and records of all expenses. You can deduct all your expenses, including the cost of any tool purchases, but only if you keep accurate records. You can get a deduction for all your expenses and the cost of any tools you purchase. However, only if you keep good records.

You can deduct rent, electricity and water as well as gas, telephone, Internet, and other expenses directly related to business activities.

Any equipment that you buy can be depreciated and in most cases the entire amount of such purchases can be deducted during the same year. Before you complete your income tax forms, it is important to verify this information with the IRS and an accountant. Turbotax

Online for Small Businesses will calculate your taxes accurately if you do all the tax preparation yourself.

It's easy to search Google for a free and simple program that will create invoices for customers if you have a need.

GoDaddy Online Accounting allows you to create and process invoices. All my invoices are processed through Paypal.com

Simply add the invoice numbers to your bank statements to identify invoices that have deposits. This is not a viable option for part-time, low-income businesses.

To save money on printing custom invoices, you can purchase generic invoices from any office supply store. The computer-generated invoices can be customized with your business information, giving them a professional look that is vital for future business.

You can save for your income taxes

Either you should arrange to pay estimated income taxes every quarter on your handyman income, or you can open a savings account where you can deposit a portion of each job to pay your income taxes. The Internal Revenue Service will send forms to you to cover estimated taxes if your business income is very high. These taxes are subject to interest and penalty charges if you fail to pay them. It is good to avoid a large tax bill at year's end by using estimated tax. This is a payroll deduction method that small businesses can use.

You Must Pay Your Taxes on Time

Whatever your method of handling income tax obligations, ensure that they are completed by the due date. You can file your tax form to request a check and submit it if you are unable or unable to pay the full amount by the due date. You will be billed.

The balance plus interest and penalty. Contact the Internal Revenue Service if you are still unable to pay. They will arrange for installments. Do not ignore them, or neglect to file your annual income tax return. They will eventually get their money, and penalties and interest will soon add up.

Some argue that cash payments received from customers should not be reported as income because there is no record. While this may

sound true, it could prove to be problematic long-term. It is up to you to decide if the risk is worth it. It may be a wise decision to not do it and could have serious consequences.

All income earned by businesses must be subject to income tax. The tax code prohibits businesses from failing to pay income taxes on all income, regardless of whether it is cash, check or credit card. Are you willing to put yourself at risk of having problems with Internal Revenue Service? This is not the same problem as when you make mistakes on your tax forms. This could lead to tax evasion or at most, interest and heavy penalties. You may also face frequent, inconvenient tax audits.

5- Accounting, Licensing and Taxes

Businesses need to be either home-based or commercial. The requirements vary from one area to the next. Before opening a business, it is important to understand the requirements in your locality. You may be surprised at the differences between communities. This could cause problems.

My business was located in Tampa, Florida. I had to obtain an occupational license. This requirement was not present in Austin. To collect the sales tax in Florida, I needed a sales tax certificate. While one community may have a different licensing requirement, both States require a certificate to collect sales tax.

I discovered that the Tangible tax, which is an annual tax on equipment value in the State, was also collected by both States. You pay not only a sales tax when your equipment is purchased, but also an annual tax on its value.

Research any taxes and licensing fees that your State and community charges businesses for operating within their borders. You will be able to save time and avoid any fines for not adhering to local laws. It is possible to operate entirely under radar in certain areas and not pay taxes or obtain licenses. However, I do not recommend this. Follow local regulations instead. Participating in the business community is better than not purchasing licenses or registering to run your business. This shows professionalism to potential customers. It will also help you to advertise your business and make your name known to the taxing agencies in your area.

The Internal Revenue Service

Many of us have paid income taxes to IRS for many years. Your income tax preparations will be easy if you work for an employer of reasonable size. The employer will deduct the taxes from your income, and give you an annual form detailing exactly what you earned during the year.

Social security and taxes. This removes many of the costs and complications involved in preparing your annual income tax returns, even if they are filed by an income tax preparation firm.

Keep track of all deductions

You must keep track of all costs when you start your business. This will allow you to deduct them from your income. You could face serious financial problems if you don't keep accurate records of your income and expenses. Quickbooks is a popular accounting software that many businesses use. It is a great software. It is important to keep your accounting system up-to-date. It is foolish to fall behind and then play catchup later. This can lead to frustration and a waste of time in the preparation of reports for your business.

Online accounting is a good option if you are a sole proprietor. GoDaddy Online Accounting is what I use and have been using it for many years. This online service is affordable, reliable, convenient, accurate, and secure.

It is essential to have separate accounts for personal and business purposes in order to use GoDaddy Online Accounting. A business checking account is required, as well as a credit card that is used only for business purposes. To accept credit card payments, you will also need a Credit Card Merchant account. After years of using them, I recommend setting up credit card processing through PayPal. It is also possible to open a business savings account.

After you have set up all these accounts, you can sign up to GoDaddy Online Accounting. They will guide you through connecting your accounts to their service. Once completed, they scan all accounts daily and keep track all income and expenses. Although the service can identify where each item should go, it is not perfect. You will need to verify that everything is correct before you sign up. Once everything is correctly identified, the service will automatically handle it. You can get reports from them at any time to manage income taxes, sales taxes, and profit and loss statements. You may be able to rely on a friend or family member to help you with these tasks. Make sure that you have all the necessary records. You are kept up to date and receive reports at least monthly on the state of your accounts. You, as the owner of the company, should always be aware of your financial position.

Part-time businesses can use a checking account for accounting

You can save money and time if you plan to only run your handyman business part-time. This can be done by opening a separate checking account for business purposes. It is a bad idea to mix business income and expenses with personal funds.

After you open your checking account, ensure that all income earned by your business is deposited to your checking account. You can use a debit or check card to pay all your business bills. It is simple to keep track of your monthly statements if all your income and expenses are managed from one account. You can also sign up online for banking to view and print all of your account information at any time.

When you get your monthly statement, reconcile it and identify the purpose for each expense. You could also create a numbering system to assign each type of expense a number. Advertising is one example.

= 1, Auto Expenses = 2, Repairs = 3, etc. You can then simply place the correct amount next to each expense and keep the statements in a folder to use at the end to calculate your taxes.

You can sign up for paperless banking to print only the portion of your monthly statement you require. This will help reduce the paper you have to keep, as banks often send extra paper and advertisements along with their statements.

Keep your records clear and concise

Whatever method you use for accounting, it is important to keep it current and keep receipts and records of all expenses. You can deduct all your expenses, including the cost of any tool purchases, but only if you keep accurate records. You can get a deduction for all your expenses and the cost of any tools you purchase. However, only if you keep good records.

You can deduct rent, electricity and water as well as gas, telephone, Internet, and other expenses directly related to business activities.

Any equipment that you buy can be depreciated and in most cases the entire amount of such purchases can be deducted during the same year. Before you complete your income tax forms, it is important to verify this information with the IRS and an accountant. Turbotax Online for Small Businesses will calculate your taxes accurately if you do all the tax preparation yourself.

It's easy to search Google for a free and simple program that will create invoices for customers if you have a need.

GoDaddy Online Accounting allows you to create and process invoices. All my invoices are processed through Paypal.com Simply add the invoice numbers to your bank statements to identify invoices that have deposits. This is not a viable option for part-time, low-income businesses.

To save money on printing custom invoices, you can purchase generic invoices from any office supply store. The computer-generated invoices can be customized with your business information, giving them a professional look that is vital for future business.

You can save for your income taxes

Either you should arrange to pay estimated income taxes every quarter on your handyman income, or you can open a savings account where you can deposit a portion of each job to pay your income taxes. The Internal Revenue Service will send forms to you to cover estimated taxes if your business income is very high. These taxes are subject to interest and penalty charges if you fail to pay them. It is good to avoid a large tax bill at year's end by using estimated tax. This is a payroll deduction method that small businesses can use.

You Must Pay Your Taxes on Time

Whatever your method of handling income tax obligations, ensure that they are completed by the due date. You can file your tax form to request a check and submit it if you are unable or unable to pay the full amount by the due date. You will be billed.

The balance plus interest and penalty. Contact the Internal Revenue Service if you are still unable to pay. They will arrange for installments. Do not ignore them, or neglect to file your annual income tax return. They will eventually get their money, and penalties and interest will soon add up.

Some argue that cash payments received from customers should not be reported as income because there is no record. While this may sound true, it could prove to be problematic long-term. It is up to you to decide if the risk is worth it. It may be a wise decision to not do it and could have serious consequences.

All income earned by businesses must be subject to income tax. The tax code prohibits businesses from failing to pay income taxes on all income, regardless of whether it is cash, check or credit card. Are you willing to put yourself at risk of having problems with Internal Revenue Service? This is not the same problem as when you make mistakes on your tax forms. This could lead to tax evasion or at most, interest and heavy penalties. You may also face frequent, inconvenient tax audits.

6- Getting Started

There are certain steps you should take to start a handyman company. Once you have resolved all tax and licensing issues and organized your vehicle and tools for customers, you are ready to attract customers to your business.

Look Professional

First, you must appear like a business to attract customers. Although you may only be a single-person company, it is important to present your business professionally in all you do. You can purchase business cards or stationery. They don't have to be costly, but they shouldn't look cheap. You will need to have all the required contract documents ready in order to be able to offer your services when you first meet your customer. It is important to prepare forms neatly and not just jot down on scrap paper.

Take photos of any work you've done for your home, friends, or family members and create a small album. This will allow you to show potential clients the images. This will show your ability to do high-quality work. Take close-ups to see the details and quality of your work.

You can use these photographs for a dual purpose. You can use them to create a website so that prospects can view your work 24 hours a days. https://godaddy.com/ has information about how to set up and manage your own website for a small business. Wix is not the only website company. You can check them out.

If you have any questions, please contact me. I will be happy to help you create a blog or website.

Get in touch with everyone!

Once you have all the pieces in place, you can start to contact everyone you know, family members and friends. You can contact them via phone, email or mail. You may find it best to contact them using more than one method. Some people prefer to be contacted personally. Let everyone know what you're doing, and ask them to share your business with their families and friends. You can give them additional business cards. Make sure it includes your website, email address, phone number, and a link to your website.

These messages should not be impersonal. It is not a good idea for you to send a generic message to all your contacts. Instead, send individual emails to each recipient and personalize them to grab their attention. Personalized emails are more likely to be opened than mass-mailed messages to a group. Although it is more work, more people will respond to your email and read it. This is crucial for your success.

To generate interest, you might start out with very low pricing and then introduce yourself to other customers who will refer you to them. This could work well as word-of-mouth advertising is the best way to find customers.

Advertising Carefully to Avoid Wasting Money

Advertising can be costly and not yield any results. Find out who your top prospects are and how to reach them. Local weekly newspapers are a good place to begin. These ads are much cheaper than daily newspapers and can be kept for a week rather than one day.

You should keep the ads in the newspaper for several weeks before you decide if they are producing results. An ad that is only seen once will rarely generate results. A similar ad for several weeks might generate interest. Keep running the ad until you have enough business. All ads should include your website address, email address, phone number, and telephone number. It should be easy for people to reach you.

7-Use the Internet

Advertising on the Internet is a great option. Make sure to mention your blog or website in every ad. With just one word, prospects will be able to find you and your photo album. You shouldn't just create your website and forget about it. Every time you complete a job, add to it. Ask for a testimonial from the owner and permission to use it in your website or album. Ask if they are willing to be referred by prospects. This could help convert a prospect to a customer. Advertising should focus on your prospect's benefits, not you. Potential customers want to know the benefits for them. Do not tell potential customers how great you are. Do not tell them how wonderful you are. Instead, highlight the benefits they get from working with you. Tell them how you are.

You will be satisfied with your job and get a fair price.

You can tell them you are aware of how hard it is to live in an apartment while you have a messy job. So, you promise to clean up after yourself so that there is no mess. You can compile a list of these benefits and include it in every sales pitch, ad or web page. Your prospects will prefer you to your competitors if you clearly present the benefits.

Everybody should have a business card

Keep your business cards handy at all times, as you never know when you might need to share information about your company with someone. Include some information about your work on your business card so you can quickly share it with others.

Make sure you are ready to impress when you have the opportunity. You should have a 30-second spiel prepared about the advantages of doing business with you so that it is easy to recall when you are asked about your company. It's impossible to predict when someone might be interested in what you do. Don't miss an opportunity to create business.

Customer retention

It is important to get customers, but it is equally important to keep them. To get a new client can be eight-ten times more expensive than keeping a customer you have. How can you keep every customer you have? Although it's not difficult, it requires some effort and understanding of human nature.

First, treat your customers with respect and show appreciation for their business. This will bring you two benefits: the customer will continue to use your services and they will refer others to you. This is crucial to your financial success. To achieve this, you must have a solid reputation for high quality work and exceptional customer service. Good impressions are what customers will recommend. It is rare to mention a person who acts in a mediocre manner.

Excellence doesn't necessarily mean that you don't make mistakes. It is a common saying, "Show me someone who makes no mistakes, and I'll show to you someone who doesn't make any mistakes." If you have many jobs,

You will make mistakes and have to fix them. Your ability to deal with mistakes can make or break a customer's perception of your excellence. Customers should see mistakes as an opportunity to impress them with your excellence. Your mistake can be corrected quickly and your customer will not be penalized for it. This will make you more productive.

A prompt apology is the most important aspect of correcting mistakes. You must apologize immediately and fix the problem at no cost to your customer. Then, move on. Although this seems straightforward, many people find it difficult to admit their mistakes and make apologies. Think back to the time you were treated poorly or badly by a merchant. Was there an apology? Did the problem get fixed the first time it was mentioned or before? If you have similar experiences to mine, an apology is something that you will always remember. This is a great opportunity to take advantage.

Even if the customer doesn't notice, you can start correcting a mistake. Do not wait to be forced into doing so. The way it is handled will surprise your customer and they will tell their friends.

Dr. Wayne Dyer refers to those who provide great customer service as eagles, and those who are less concerned about customer service as ducks. When I receive excellent service, I tell my friends and inform them that I found an eagle who helped me. Eagles are very rare, and you can have one in your business. Your customers will be happy to tell others about you.

Don't worry about being right if you want to serve your customers better. Your business will suffer financially if you think that being right is more important than being right. The most important thing when things go wrong in a business transaction is how the customer feels after the event. If you make a mistake, even if it's a major one, you can admit it and apologize quickly. Your customer will be just as proud of you as if the incident never occurred. You will convince your customer that you value their business. They can count on you to provide honest service and good value. This will keep them coming back to you and referring others to your services. If the customer feels that he has been satisfied with the business transaction, you have done your job correctly.

Or she should return to you next time they require a similar service. Customer service is a win-win situation. Before you make a decision about customer service, think about your customer. Consider how you would treat someone in the same situation.

8- How to Use Your Computer and The Internet

When this book was published in 2009, computers were not essential tools for operating a handyman business. It is today, I believe it is. It makes many tasks much easier and allows you to keep in touch with your customers and prospects. Many ways computers can help you achieve financial success are discussed in this chapter.

Since I am a computer user, the information about computer use has been limited to what can be done on a computer and the software that is available. You can do almost anything with a Mac, however. Finding the right software is all that's required. Some people using Mac computers will already know which software to use, but others will need to search Google, Yahoo or another search engine to find the best programs.

Business Accounting and Income Tax Preparation

Your computer is your best tool for business accounting. I recommend downloading Quickbooks Simple Accounting, a free program that you can download in 2009. This program was sufficient for most small businesses. It can be upgraded at a moderate cost to become a full-featured business application.

These days, things have changed and I don't believe that this free version exists. Online accounting seems to be the new trend. I have been using it for over five years. GoDaddy bought the company I started with and I have been with them for many years. GoDaddy Online Accounting is not a company that I am interested in financially, but they are a service I highly recommend based on personal experience. They will handle your accounting and invoicing for you as a one-person business for only ten bucks per month. Quickbooks offers affordable online accounting services. They are also a reputable and professional company.

The computer can also be used to prepare your income tax forms. Turbotax Online is my favorite income tax preparation application. There are many options, but it's the easiest and most useful. You can do all your taxes online using an internet connection. The interview process is simple and easy to follow. This virtually guarantees that you will complete your taxes correctly and receive every deduction. Turbotax Online is available at:

http://turbotax.com

These links cannot be used because this book is paperback. You will need to type them in the address bar of your browser (Internet Explorer, Firefox etc.) Should you experience problems please email me at bill@positive-imaging.com and I will assist you with an email link in reply.

Photo Album and Creation of a Web Site

You can use either an Android Smartphone or iPhone to take job photos. These photos can be saved or sent to your computer for use on your site. After completing an outstanding job, you can instantly create pictures. Edit only what you need and save the rest.

You can use the same images to create your web site on Wix or GoDaddy.

These are some things you should keep in mind when creating your web site.

1.Resize all of your photos to display on a phone or monitor. Because they are meant for high quality printing, photo files can sometimes be large. This quality is not possible for monitors so details are lost. Even worse, large files can take longer to open which means that your potential customers will wait to see your photos. Because of our short attention spans, people are more likely to abandon your website if it takes too much time to open. This issue can be avoided by resizing images for the web.

2.Keep in mind that your website should focus on the customer's benefits. While it is okay to give customers a little bit of information about you, the focus must be on what they get. What can they expect from you that they don't get from other companies?

3. Create a professional-looking web site. It should be simple to read and contain lots of white space. For those who prefer to scroll through websites, you can tell your story using short headings. This will allow them to find what they are looking for and allows those who wish to learn more access the full story. It is important to explain the different types of work you accept, and any

specialties. Anyone who is willing to spend the time to learn about how to do it should be able.

Blogs

You can help them complete their task quickly, competently, and reliable.

A blog is a better choice than a website. They are easier to maintain and update. Blogs are interactive, so prospects and customers can communicate with them.

Smartphones

The smartphone was a new concept when this book was published. But it's now a common tool for displaying all your work. A gallery of images of your work can be accessed from your smartphone, as well as a mobile access to your website. You should take full advantage of this feature, but remember to also keep the old information handy as many people don't have smartphones.

Keep in touch with prospects and customers

The computer can be a great tool for keeping in touch with customers and prospects. Email can be a great tool to maintain a close relationship and build trust with people who are interested in your company. Be careful not to spam, as it can turn people away from your business and make them less likely to become customers. You can request permission to send emails via forms on your website or simply ask people you know if they would like information.

Small and large businesses alike use Outlook as their local email client. There are many options for managing your email. You may already have one that works well. Google is the best place to get an email setup. You can set up your email with ease and get many additional features, such as a calendar and other useful amenities. If you don't already have something better, I recommend using a Gmail account to manage all your business email.

Access to email from any location is key. Outlook should be linked to a Windows Live Hotmail account if you use it as an email client. This will allow you to access your email from anywhere you are.

Many businesses use texting to communicate with their customers via smartphones. You might find texting useful. Texting is something I use very rarely.

Because I don't like the small keyboard, but that's me.

Back up your computer

It is essential that you have a backup plan in place if you intend to use your computer to run your business. You can have your data stored in a secure location so that it is available for you in case your computer crashes or you need to buy a new one.

External hard drives are the best way to back up your files. Because they are small and portable, I recommend that you get one that is laptop-compatible. When you are planning your backup program, remember that backup means two copies. Many people think they are backing up files because they use an external drive or flash drive. You must have a backup copy of your files on your computer's hard drive and another copy on an external hard drive.

My computer is an essential tool in all of my business activities. It is used for everything: accounting, web design, publishing books, editing photos, marketing, and email. It is a must-have tool for any business.

An online backup service is a good option if you're not sure if a backup will be effective. I have used Backblaze for several years and recommend them at http://backblaze.com. For sixty dollars a year they will backup unlimited data on your computer and any external drives.

- What to Charge and Why

It is crucial to set the right price for each job. This can be difficult due to the numerous variables. Two things are required to ensure that prices are set accurately. First, you must set a price that is low enough to make your job competitive. Second, it must not be too high to make sure that your business activities are profitable. Although there are simple methods to calculate the cost of any job, regardless of its complexity, it is best to start small and leave the more difficult jobs to more experienced people. It can be costly to get in over your head without enough experience. There are many factors to consider depending on the job and the customer.

What are you willing to make?

Ask yourself this question: "How much do you want to be paid for my time?" This hourly rate applies to all jobs, except in exceptional circumstances which will be discussed later. This amount should not include any expenses and be paid before taxes. This figure does not include overhead or materials costs.

It is crucial to get paid for your time. I've met self-employed people who claim that they make a lot of money from a particular job. I find it surprising how high the profit is relative to the cost of the job. It becomes apparent that they don't really mean profit when they tell me this. Their definition of profit is the money left after they have paid for the materials. They tell me how much they earned, and I ask them how much they paid. This is not the best way to run your business. Profit is the net amount after subtracting all expenses for the job, including labor. The labor cost in a solo business is the amount you pay yourself. Profit is defined as the difference between the total cost of the job and the cost for materials.

When you have determined how much you are willing to work for each hour, you can add that cost to the labor cost of every job.

The Hourly Figure

When setting an hourly rate for yourself to be paid, it is important to keep in mind both reality and your desire. While you desire to be paid the most money for your time, it is important to balance what you can afford with what is available in the local market.

CNN News reported that the average handyman's hourly income was $17.40 in 2009. This was an average, based on some research. It suggested that you use a slightly higher figure of $20.00/hour as a starting point for some useful calculations. The rate should be higher considering that it has been eight years since the last time this was done. However, wages have remained flat due to the economic turmoil that the country has experienced. It is worth doing some research to find out what the charges are in your area.

Keep in mind that figures may not include labor. What you want to establish is a cost for your labor. It is possible to get more, but it may also be too expensive. The hourly rate must be determined for your job cost calculations. You can make it higher or lower depending on your personal preference. There is no wrong answer as long as you're being realistic.

Another thing to establish is how many hours you will work each month. For simplicity sake, you should start with 160 hours. This amounts to four 40-hour weeks per month, or 48 weeks each year. You may be unable to work for four weeks due to illness, vacation, or other reasons.

However, this doesn't necessarily mean you will work the exact same number of hours every month. You may initially be working more. This gives you a base for pricing your work. The average rate for labor in Austin, Texas is $35.00 to $80 an hour with $55.00 being the average. Take some time to determine what is most effective in your area.

How to Buy and Maintain Your Tools

Next, consider the cost of your tools. A fair number of tools are required for home repairs. The entire list was covered in Chapter Three. You may have many of the tools you need. You must consider whether you have all the tools or need to buy them. You can find out more.

They must also be kept in top working order. They may need to be replaced if they become worn or if they are unable to perform as well as they used to.

If you want to make a living as a handyman, all of these costs should be taken into consideration. Depreciation is the process by which equipment ages and needs to be replaced. To pay for new equipment, you must create a depreciation plan for your tools.

You can also depreciate tools to reduce your tax liability. This allows you to deduct the costs from your gross income, thereby reducing your taxes. The depreciation schedule must be followed even after a tool is depreciated entirely for income tax purposes. This will ensure that funds are available to replace the tools.
This can be done by calculating an annual depreciation rate based on the cost of your tools and how long you expect them to last. Let's say your tools have a total value of $4,800.00. They are then depreciated every five years at $960.00 per annum. Divide $960.00 by 12, for a total of
$80.00 per month for maintenance and replacement of tools. Divide the $80.00 figure by 160 hours and you will get $.50 an hour.
Work vehicle
You will need a vehicle to handle your home repairs. Just like other equipment, the actual vehicle cost is covered by depreciation. Let's say your vehicle costs $18,000.00, and you expect it will last five years. Let's say that your vehicle is worth $3,000.00 after five years. Automobiles have a resale price. That leaves $15,000.00 to be depreciated over five years. Divide the
Divide $15,000.00 by 60 Months and then divide this sum by 160 Hours. This gives you an hourly rate of $1.56
***NOTICE:** It is possible to depreciate the entire amount in the first tax year, but it is still important that*
Add this number to your bank account and deposit the funds. You will eventually need to replace the vehicle. The ability to have the funds will prevent you from having to finance another vehicle.

How to maintain and fuel your vehicle

Good records are essential for determining your fuel and maintenance costs. To keep track of your expenses, you can buy a small journal for auto maintenance and fuel at any office supply shop. This task will be handled by an app on your smartphone in 2020. Let's say it costs $1.
$300.00 per month to maintain your vehicle and keep it fueled. This would be $1.88 an hour.

Insurance at a High Price

Insurance is another expensive item you should consider. You and your vehicle require adequate insurance to cover you and your passengers in the event of an accident, theft, or damage. In most states, insurance coverage is required. This is just one aspect of insurance. This is where you'll need to make an important decision. Handymen can work without insurance. They can charge less for their services and save money for customers. This may seem like a great deal for both the handyman and the customer, but it's only true if there is no problem during a job.

Our litigious society means that if something is damaged or someone is injured accidentally, the first stop is usually an attorney's office. It is possible to end up with a very serious legal problem that will cost you far more than you can afford.

Uninsured handymen are not much better. You can sue the homeowner if you are hurt by an unforeseeable problem with your home. Although the homeowner may be able to reverse the situation, it is still a serious problem.

These problems can be solved by liability insurance. It covers you, your company, and your work site. These policies can be very expensive if you don't shop well. Insurance agents will attempt to sell you too much insurance.

It's possible to have too much coverage, but it's not a good idea.

You don't want to spend too much on coverage. I am not an expert in insurance so I recommend you speak with an experienced agent and ensure that they are familiar with your needs.

Although you won't actually use it, it will look great on your ads and homeowners won't be tempted to hire an uninsured company for home repairs.

Another important consideration is your health insurance. You will have to buy it, even if your spouse works in an industry that offers insurance benefits. For self-employed people, this one expense can cause a lot of headaches. This is even when you consider the Affordable Healthcare Act.

I recommend that you have at least some major medical insurance coverage. Keep the deductible high enough so that premiums are affordable. You will not be able get all of this insurance for less that $390 per month, which would require an additional $2.45 per-hour cost.

Keep track of all your taxes

Federal income taxes can be a problem for many. Taxes are something you have to face if you want to be a business owner. It's not unusual for small businesses to encounter problems with the Internal Revenue Service. Their job is to collect federal income tax. The problem is usually caused by failing to make sufficient provisions and set aside funds for income tax payments.

The IRS can cause serious problems and can prove costly. Failure to pay taxes on time can result in interest and penalties which can quickly double, or even triple, your tax obligations.

Pay your taxes quarterly if you can, as the Internal Revenue Service requires. You can open a savings account to set aside a portion of your income for taxes each April 15th. At least 10% of your gross income should be saved, and more if possible. Although ten percent of your gross income is significant, it is necessary to pay your income taxes on a timely basis. Although it is hard to determine the exact amount of income taxes you will pay, it is likely that between twenty and thirty percent of your net income will be taxed.

Social security alone accounts for 15% of your income. This is because you, as an independent worker, must pay all costs of Social Security. The company pays the rest. Employees pay about 7 and 1 1/2 percent of Social Security.

An annual net income of $30,000.00 could lead to a cost of $8,000.00 including Social Security Taxes. This would also include the cost for Income Taxes. The amount you can deduct will vary depending on what deductions you have, but it is better to save more than less. It is going into savings, so any extra can be used to increase your investments, or for vacations or other purposes. Last note: Don't forget about State income taxes.

You are responsible for all your work

You will be the sole proprietor of your business and responsible for estimating each job, preparing bid presentations, picking materials up, running errands, and all other tasks that take up a lot time. It is important that you get paid for your time to ensure fair profits. It's difficult to charge customers for the time they spend on jobs before they actually happen. This time must be included in your hourly calculation. For an hourly rate of $1.88, you will need to add $300 each month.

Profit is not to be forgotten

Two ways can you calculate your job profit. You can either make the profit portion of the hourly rate or you can do the other. The other option, which I recommend, is to calculate it separately, based on the whole job. In either case, you should calculate profit at least 25%. Because it allows for profit on the materials, the more popular way to increase profit is to base it on the total cost of the job.

Now you have a basic list with all the numbers required to calculate the cost of any job. These are just examples. These are just examples of how the formula works. However, you will need to calculate the best area figures for each job in order to determine the right pricing.

The chart below shows the breakdown of hourly fees. It calculates

The hourly rate can be figured by listing all items mentioned previously. You should not forget that costs in your local area may differ, and that you might have other priorities. This chart is only an example and you can create your own.

How Much To Charge Chart

Hourly Wage (You decide this amount)	$ 55.00
Tool Maintenance ($80 by 160 hours)	$ .50
Vehicle ($15,000 cost/60 months by 160)	$1.56
Vehicle Maintenance and Fuel	$1.88
Insurance ($390.00 by 160 hours)	$2.45
Taxes ($8,000/12 months by 160 hours)	$4.20
Misc. Overhead ($300 by 160 hours)	$1.88
TOTAL PER HOUR	**$ 67.47**
Profit - Hourly Basis (25% of Total Per Hour)	$ 16.87
TOTAL PER HOUR INCLUDING PROFIT	**$ 84.34**

To get started, let's round off the **Total Per Hour** figure to **$68.oo** and the **Total Including Profit** figure to **$85.00** per hour.

Now let's go through a couple of sample jobs so you can see exactly how to use this information to come up with accurate pricing that will ensure you make a profit on every job.

Sample Job One

For the purposes of the first sample job, let's assume that it will take 16 hours to complete the entire job. Just multiply 16 times $85.00 for a total of $1,360.00. This is your total labor and profit on this job.

The next step is to calculate the cost of the materials. Start by using your job information to prepare a precise materials list. This list should include the quantity of each item. Strive for accuracy here because any mistakes will come right out of your pocket. Even though many home repair jobs may not be material intensive, any material costs must be accounted for or your profits will be reduced. Assign an accurate price to each item and, if in doubt, price the item higher rather then lower. You may need to contact some suppliers to get updated prices.

Let's assume the materials will cost $270.00. Add the labor cost amount of $1,360.00 to the $270.00 for materials for a total of $1,630.00, which is the total price of the job.

If you prefer to add the profit separately, use the $68.00 per hour figure times 16 and that equals $1,088.00. Then add the $270.00 for materials for a total of $1,358.00. Calculate twenty five percent of $1,358.00 and it equals

$339.50. Add that to $1,358.00 for a total $1,697.50. Notice that the figures from both methods are close but the second figure is higher. You may consider this difference to your advantage on those jobs that require tighter pricing to be more competitive.

There is Always Some Waste

Remember to add a waste factor. When you are calculating jobs realize that some waste will be encountered. You will probably have to buy more material than you actually need because of this. The cost of this additional material must be covered in the job.

Sample Job Two

This time it will be a material intensive job that takes only 10 hours but requires $475.00 for the materials. Start by determining the hourly labor and related expense cost by multiplying 10 by our $85.00 per hour rate for a total of $850.00. Next, we add the cost of materials and come up with a total price for the job of $1,325.00 including profit.

Now check it using the method where we add the profit to the full amount of the job including the materials. For this we multiply 10 times $68.00 for a total labor and expense cost of $680.00. Then we add $475.00 for the materials to this for a total job cost of $1,155.00 not including profit. Using the twenty five percent profit formula, we multiply twenty-five percent times

$1,155.00 and come up with a profit amount of $288.75. We add the profit to the $1,155.00 for a total job price of $1,443.75.

Notice that this price is close but higher than the price with the profit calculated as part of the labor. Compare the two sample jobs and notice that in both sample jobs the price with the profit added separately is higher. Once again, this difference can assist you in competitive situations by providing price options that could help you get the job.

The most important thing to remember is that all of these prices would leave you a profit if your time and material cost were calculated correctly. Even though the prices are different, they would all work out fine. So, how do you decide which price to use? This requires some intuitive thinking when you are speaking with your customer.

The correct price is the one the customer is willing to pay. If it seems that the customer is ready to give you the job, go with the higher price. If you feel like the customer may be calling someone else and it may become competitive, go with the lower price to increase the odds that you will get the job.

Don't Forget The Backlog

Consider your backlog of jobs when calculating prices. If a lot of work has been coming in and you are quite busy at the time, go with the higher price. If things have been slow and you could use the work, go with the lower price.

Either way, you will get paid for your time and make a profit. As time passes, your comfort level in the business increases and you become more aware of how a prospect may react to your price. This will help you decide what to do in each case.

A Final Check of Your Pricing

Since accuracy in setting prices is so important, there is a way to do one final check of your price on your first few jobs. Exactly how this check is handled depends on the complexity of the job and also on whether it is labor or material intensive.

This method should only be used to check your pricing, not to actually calculate a final job price. This is because there are too many variables involved in the process.

The first variable is to determine if the job is material intensive. For example, if the material costs comprise a large percentage of the calculations, you would use a ratio between 2.5 and 4 for your calculations. However, if the material costs are a small part of the total job, as in the job we used as the first sample, you could use a ratio as high as 6.

The second variable is complexity. If the job is relatively straightforward and you expect no major difficulties, the above ratios are fine. If the level of difficulty seems high, you could adjust the ratio by one or two before using it. Remember that this is only a backup to your normal method of calculating job prices as already described.

While this may sound complex, remember that it only serves to ease your mind about the accuracy of your pricing. You have already taken the time to properly calculate a price for the job. Once you get accustomed to pricing jobs, this final step is unnecessary.

The ratio numbers are used to multiply times the cost of materials. For example, in the first sample job the cost of materials is 270.00, the job is labor intensive, and it seems to be of average complexity so we would multiply by 6 giving a total of $1,620.00.

In the second sample job the cost of materials is $475.00, it is material intensive and the work is relatively simple so we would multiply by 3 giving a total of $1,425.00 indicating that our pricing is quite safe.

There is yet another way to take advantage of this additional information. You will run into homeowners who wish to negotiate and may make you a counter offer. With this figure in mind, you might consider accepting a counter offer close to this amount because your have tested your pricing thoroughly.

This improves your chances of getting jobs even when the homeowner considers your pricing a little high. It's not necessary to do all of these

methods to establish your pricing but it allows you many options to ensure you will make money on every job.
Please remember these figures are not necessarily accurate for your area. You will have to do research to determine the prices of all items for your jobs.
Determine what is considered a fair wage for the kind of work you will be doing. The cost of living in your community may be much higher and therefore the income for home repair experts may also be higher. Research this thoroughly so you don't short change yourself or overcharge and lose jobs.

The Grief Factor

You may not hear about this in any other information about the home repair business but I believe it is critically important. It was of real help to me over the many years I spent doing home repair, home remodeling, and woodworking.

As your business grows, many interesting people will be encountered. Most of them simply want a good job and as long as you deliver that everything will work out well with them. On the other hand, you will run into prospects and customers who are impossible to please and will make things miserable for you no matter how good your work. It's important to recognize and make advance adjustments for this kind of customer.

It isn't difficult to identify these potential customers and you must do it during the initial contact, before you agree to do the job. You can identify them in various ways.

ŸThey will take an hour to explain something that most people will explain in five or ten minutes.

ŸThey will convey all the terrible experiences they have had with other home repair companies or contractors in vivid detail.

ŸThey will continuously repeat that they can't afford the work unless the price is extremely low.

ŸEven for a simple job, you will waste much more time with them than with any of your other prospects.

In short, it will be obvious that working with them will not be pleasant, hence the grief. In these situations I strongly suggest one of two methods to deal with these potential customers.

ŸExplain that you don't take on the specific kind of work they want done and leave as quickly as possible.

ŸAfter calculating your price, think about how much trouble they will be causing for you as the job progresses and add a substantial percentage to the price of the work.

Either of these methods will protect you. In one case, you will not have to deal with an unpleasant situation. On the other hand, if you get the job, you will get paid well for putting up with the grief. Your preference may be to leave but for enough money you might put up with a lot.

Years ago I spent over an hour with a potential customer and by the end of that time I knew that it would be unbearable to do the job. I couldn't say that I did not do that kind of work because they were familiar with my work. Instead, I calculated the job normally and then doubled that price. I thought the prospect was going to have a fainting spell and I did not get the job. Maybe that wasn't a nice thing to do but I have always tried to enjoy my work and it was obvious that I would not have enjoyed that job.

You will have to make these decisions yourself and if one gets by you, it will be a valuable experience to guide you in dealing with future problem prospects.

The Rule of Supply and Demand

The rule of supply and demand is one of the most important rules of business. Small business owners often lose out on additional money they could be making for the same amount of work by overlooking this important rule.

Your prices should always reflect the demand for your work. This is common practice in many businesses.

Check hotel rates during peak and slow seasons to see how they vary. You can also check airfares during various times of the year. When there is low demand, the prices go down to encourage more people to buy. When the demand is high, the prices go up to increase profits and adjust the demand to the available supply.

You can take advantage of the rule of supply and demand as a one-person business. When you have a backlog of work and continue getting more jobs than you can possibly do in a reasonable amount of time, increase your prices until the work levels off to a flow rate that you can handle. The formula for how much to charge, in the previous pages, indicates pricing to ensure that you make a living. The main purpose of the formula is to make sure that you charge enough so you never lose money while making at least a small profit. It does not indicate how much you may charge for a job if it is sold to someone who knows your work and is willing to pay more to have you do their job.

The actual amount that you can charge is determined by a customer's willingness to pay, not by any formula. The right price for anything is the amount a willing buyer will pay a willing seller. Beyond that, there are no limits. Some people quarrel with this and dub it gouging. That might be the case if you are taking advantage of a desperate situation like a flood, hurricane, tornado, etc. But under normal circumstances, the market for services sets the real prices and there is no reason you should not participate in the market, even on a small scale.

It often seems that there is a preconceived notion that a self-employed person can only make wages and must be prepared to sacrifice a decent income, medical benefits and vacations to do the work he or she loves. Do you really believe that? If you do, it may well be true for you. If you know any individuals who are trying to make a living with the work they love, this may be the case for them. It doesn't have to be that way for you. If you have the skills to do a good job and charge enough for it, you can make a good living as a self-employed home repair expert.

I graduated from the home repair business into a full-time woodworking business and learned a great deal in that process. One of the truly important lessons that helped me make much more money was about perceived value and the law of supply and demand. Years ago I wrote some notes on that subject and I believe they will be helpful to anyone wishing to be in the home repair business. Those notes begin below.

NOTES ON PERCEIVED VALUE AND SUPPLY AND DEMAND

After many years in the woodworking business I learned never to limit myself by what the competition charged. As my backlog increased, I began to raise my prices and found that even people who did not know me personally were willing to pay me more for jobs because of the reputation I had developed. You may also be worth much more to your customers.

Some people are making $10.00 per hour while others make well over

$100.00 per hour. There may be a significant difference in skills but what often makes the difference is the value a customer perceives. A clear example of this is the art world. One canvas may look beautiful and not be worth the cost of the canvas materials to buyers. Another canvas of the same size may look worthless to you or me and bring thousands, even millions from art lovers. This is all value perceived by the customer who is willing and able to pay the price.

The same thing is applicable to woodworkers. There are woodworkers who struggle to get a few hundred dollars for a really nice rocking chair and others who are getting thousands for a similar chair. And, the one that is getting thousands has a long waiting list. Perhaps one of those woodworkers is much more skilled than the other but more likely they are at similar skill levels. Perceived value is the key ingredient. One of the woodworkers has become famous, perhaps because of books he has written or some other public exposure.

Whatever the reason, his work is perceived to have more value. Use perceived value to your advantage. If people really love your work, then charge as much as the market will bear.

If you want to be in business in a free enterprise system such as ours, you must remember that the price of everything is based on supply and demand. The maximum price of any product or service is the maximum amount that a customer is willing to pay for it. If you have a problem with the idea of perceived value and supply and demand and believe that it is somehow unfair to charge more based simply on demand, remember that this will limit your profit significantly.

Making a good living in home repair requires that you consistently charge as much as possible for all of your jobs. Considering perceived value and supply and demand will help you do that.

4 - Contracting Jobs

You will need job contract forms but keep them simple because customers are hesitant to sign long, complex, difficult to understand forms written in legalese. On the other hand, your contract must protect you in the event a problem arises during a job.

Keep in mind that a good contract is an agreement between two honest people who want to do business with each other. If one or the other intends to cheat on the agreement, the contract will not resolve all issues. It may protect you to some extent but it won't stop problems from arising if you do not perform as agreed or if there is a misunderstanding between you and the owner.

This means that even with a good contract, being right is not the important thing. The most critical thing is to always complete your jobs in accordance with your agreement leaving happy and satisfied customers who will call you again and recommend you to their friends and family.

The Steps of Contracting For Work

The first critical step involves selling the customer the idea that you are the best person to do the work. Part of that will involve finding out exactly what they want and this requires listening carefully to the prospect.

Never underestimate the importance of listening. Too many people spend valuable listening time figuring out how they are going to respond. Instead, listen intently and take notes to develop a clear understanding of your prospect's desires. Once a job is clear to you, it may be necessary to prepare some simple drawings to ensure that both you and the potential customer understand what the job involves. In some cases, a simple listing of tasks is adequate. Do whatever it takes to ensure that everything is understood by both parties before calculating the cost of the job and giving the customer a firm quote or estimate.

After this is complete, if the customer decides to proceed with the work, you can prepare the contract form. The contract should define the job using the notes that you created with the prospect and should refer to any drawings, task list, or specifications prepared for the job. All of these forms should be attached to the contract form. At this point you sign the contract and give it to the customer to sign.

The Deposit

Now comes one of the most important and often overlooked part of the contracting process. Unless you are dealing with a small job that can be completed in less than one day, every contract should require a deposit payable before the work begins. Some will tell you that it is difficult, and often impossible, to get a deposit from customers. That isn't true and you will get little resistance from anyone who trusts you enough to spend the money for the job, unless they have doubts about your honesty. If such doubts exist, you are better off without the job.

Even when you are first starting, it is no problem to get a deposit as long as you present yourself professionally, carefully explain the work, present clear and concise information about the job, a fair price, and a simple contract form. When people realize that you are serious and know what you are doing, they will not resist the deposit. Once you develop a reputation it will be even easier to obtain a deposit from your customers.

As was indicated earlier, a contract with a customer is based on trust. If a customer is unwilling to sign a contract and give you a deposit, then trust doesn't exist and the customer is concerned that you will not follow through and perform as promised.

Should you proceed without the deposit, you won't be certain that you will get paid. The deposit is a compromise. The customer has a reasonable assurance that you will do the work in order to get the rest of the money. You have a reasonable assurance you will get paid the balance because the owner has contracted with you and given you a good faith deposit that he or she will not want to lose. If even this limited amount of trust doesn't exist, it is probably in your best interest, and that of your prospect, not to proceed with the job.

With home repair the amount of the deposit can vary. On jobs that don't involve materials or can be completed in less than a full day, no deposit is necessary. On larger jobs a fifty percent deposit is appropriate.

You can make exceptions for customers like rental property owners who give you work regularly and simply pay your invoices when submitted.

At a minimum, you should normally get a deposit in an amount at least equal to the cost of the materials for any job. This way, even if something does go wrong, you would not be out of pocket for the materials.

No matter the form of your contract, you will probably run into potential customers who absolutely refuse to pay a deposit. Treat the deposit requirement as standard policy that you do not bypass for anyone. I suggest you create a deposit policy covering any job that takes more than one day or cost over a certain amount. You can determine the amount you are comfortable with. Potential customers who resist the deposit may sometimes come up with various alternatives including lower percentages or depositing the money for the job in an escrow account.

It is best to reject any scenario that precludes obtaining a fair deposit before starting the work. It is also important to give deposit checks time to clear the bank before beginning the work to avoid issues with bad checks. With the speed of present electronic banking, this will seldom take more than a day or two.

On smaller jobs you can offer the customer the alternative of purchasing all the material for the job. If necessary, they can go with you to the supplier or home improvement store and pay for everything thereby precluding any financial risk on your part.

Maintaining an adequate deposit policy is the only way to make certain you do not lose money on jobs.

Credit Cards

It is simple to set up to accept credit cards and it's especially important for small jobs even though it also works for larger jobs. There are many companies with whom you can set up but I recommend PayPal with whom I have been dealing for many years. Their rates are reasonable and you only pay if you process transactions. There are no monthly minimums. Check them out at http://paypal.com.

Dealing With General Contractors

Your deposit policy will eliminate almost all general contractors as customers. There may be remodeling contractors who want to have some work done as part of a large remodeling job and they want to pay you after they get a draw from the bank financing the work. This can be a slippery slope that can cost you a lot of money.

Some contractors try to cut prices after the work is finished because they realize the remodeling job is costing more than they estimated. If you stick with your policy, only contractors who have the financial ability to pay the deposit up front will do business with you and your odds of collecting the balance when the job is done are greatly increased.

Sometimes You Don't Need A Contract or Deposit

There are some situations where a contract or deposit arrangement may not be possible or necessary. One of those involves doing work for government agencies. In those cases, it is unlikely that you will not get paid and it may not be possible for them to arrange a deposit or even sign a contract. In most cases governments work with a purchase order arrangement and you will have to accept that if you choose to do work for them.

Deposits could also be a problem when working with large corporations. They also work with purchase orders so you may have to pass on the deposit if you want their business. You should be very careful here because some people who run corporations simply don't care about their vendors and it may take a long time to finally collect for your work.

The important thing is to handle these situations carefully always making certain you collect for every job you do. If they fail to pay you for one job, for any reason, drop them immediately until you have been paid in full. This is the only way to ensure that your business will be a financial success.

Forms You Can Use

You may consider getting an attorney to prepare a simple contract but don't allow it to become a 10 to 20 page nightmare of legal jargon. This will just make it more difficult to sell jobs.

The contract and other forms you need are not difficult to create and are similar to what would be used by a woodworking business. A sample set of forms is not included in ebook version of this book but you can download an editable set of these forms on the web at:

http://home-repair-business.com/forms/contract.rtf

http://home-repair-business.com/forms/letterhead.rtf

http://home-repair-business.com/forms/specifications.rtf

The advantage of the .rtf forms on this web site is that you can easily edit them with your company name and address. Even though these forms have worked effectively for years, there is no legal adequacy implied or guaranteed as the author is not an attorney. Using these forms will save you the time of creating your own.

5 - Getting Help

The simplest way to operate a handyman business is by accepting only home repair that you can complete on your own as a one-person business. For me, that's always been the best choice but as business grows you may be interested in doing more and larger jobs by getting some help.

The one-person business leads to financial success with the lowest possible risk and this book is geared specifically to that form of business. There are many reasons to avoid hiring employees, not the least of which is that it could complicate your life and even take the joy out of your work.
Hiring employees also creates a significantly more complex income tax situation and employees can increase the cost of your work significantly.
Obviously there will be times when you need help because you have too much work or for jobs that are too large to handle alone. Hiring subcontractors is a better way to deal with excess workloads.
Choose subcontractors carefully because they will be representing you on every job and you don't want them to harm your valuable reputation.
Don't hire a subcontractor unless you are familiar with his or her work and reputation.

What Is A Subcontractor?

Using subcontractors is definitely an excellent way to handle more jobs, but make certain you avoid subverting Internal Revenue Service payroll deduction requirements by considering employees subcontractors. You can experience serious and costly issues with the Internal Revenue Service for applying the term subcontractor incorrectly in an effort to avoid employee payroll deduction and Social Security requirements.
The Internal Revenue Service has certain requirements that must be met in order to consider someone a subcontractor. Fail to meet those requirements and your "subcontractor" will be considered an employee and you will be required to pay payroll taxes and Social Security payments that you did not deduct, plus interest, and significant penalties.
You can safely avoid such problems with the Internal Revenue Service by meeting certain specific

standards. These standards are fairly basic and include:

ŸThe subcontractor must have a business identity. That is, they must have an address, phone number and some past business experience with other customers.

ŸThe subcontractor must control his or her own hours. If you have someone working for you during certain hours that you control and you pay him or her on an hourly basis, that person is an employee to the Internal Revenue Service.

Calling someone who does not meet these basic standards a subcontractor will not impress the Internal Revenue Service. If they check on you and find this kind of situation, this person will be deemed an employee and this will hurt you financially.

Day Laborers

Naturally, if you only need someone for one day to help you perform certain tasks on a specific job, you can hire a day worker and pay him or her for that day only without consequence. However, if you need help everyday, make certain that the persons who help you can be legally considered subcontractors.

In most communities there are places to pick up day laborers and this will usually work out fine. However, if you know someone or, if your handyman business is part time, you may find a friend or coworker to assist you.

This creates a more comfortable work environment and you can confidently leave someone at a customer's home without worrying about the potential consequences of a stranger in a customer’s home.

6 - Safety

Safety is the most important topic in any book about businesses requiring the use of power tools and it's in your best interest to adhere to all safety rules. If you have all your fingers and body parts after years of using power tools, it's probably because you realize the importance of giving every power tool your full and undivided attention before turning it on.

POWER TOOLS ARE INHERENTLY DANGEROUS! Any tool that can

cut wood can also cut skin and bone. Please keep this in mind every time you use a power tool. Here are a few simple suggestions that will help you avoid injuries:

- l Plan every cut carefully before starting the tool. This is a common oversight. Instead of just jumping in and starting a cut, determine exactly what you are going to do and what problems might be posed by the procedure.
  - ŸAnother part of planning is to visualize the complete procedure before you start. This will help you avoid potential kickbacks or other injury causing incidents.
- l Clamp work pieces securely before cutting, routing or sanding. It is much quicker and easier to just hold the piece down with one hand while making the cut or routing the edge with the other but you are significantly increasing the risk of injury.
- l Read and adhere to the safety guidelines that came with the power tool. These guidelines are written to help you avoid serious injuries. It only takes a few minutes to read through the small booklets that come with power tools.
- l If you are using a power tool with one hand, always check the location of your other hand before starting the tool. That may sound silly to some but it is definitely a good way to keep all your fingers. Taking a few moments to do this will ensure that your other hand is in a safe location to avoid possible injury.
- l Never use power tools if you are tired, taking medications or using alcohol or drugs. This is a sure way to get hurt.
- l Never use a power tool while someone is talking to you or distracting you in any way. It only takes a split second for a serious injury to change your life. If someone interrupts you while using a power

tool, stop the tool and tell them it is dangerous to distract you until the tool is turned off.

1 Always use ear and eye protection and dust masks while using power tools.

Don't let lack of attention or a moment of carelessness ruin your livelihood and perhaps your life. Think before turning on any power tool and take good care of yourself and others around you.

7 - Final Notes

After more than twenty five years of doing almost every kind of home repair and woodworking project, there are few things in these businesses that I have not experienced. I retired from woodworking to write and publish books and this gives me the opportunity to share my first hand experiences. This last chapter contains a few final notes that you may find valuable. In addition to these notes, I welcome hearing from you about your own experiences and any questions that come up for you. Please email me at: bill@positive-imaging.com and I will respond as promptly as possible. Thanks again for purchasing this book.

Become An Expert

To be really profitable it helps to be a recognized expert in your chosen field. People respect experts and are more likely to trust one to do their job. Strive to be the best home repair expert in your area. That's not as difficult as it may seem. Look around and see how many people really excel at their chosen profession. Over the years I've found that most people, including handymen, simply do little more than what is absolutely required. This should make it obvious that all around you mediocrity reigns supreme. This means that if you simply excel at your work and perform well for all your customers, you will quickly establish a reputation as a highly competent and reliable expert. This also means that people will be willing to pay more for your services because of this reputation.

Develop Your Communication Skills

Those in the top five percent of their field are in demand and are paid the most. What does it take to be in that top five percent? There are two very basic things you must do to attain that status. First, you must have, or take the time to develop, excellent communications skills. That means being able to get your message across clearly to everyone, especially potential customers.

Having those skills puts you head and shoulders above most other home repair experts.

If you don't have those skills, work to improve your vocabulary and your communications skills. There are colleges, adult education programs and even home study courses to help you with this. If there is a toastmaster's club near you, join it to improve your rapport with the public.

Are you wondering what this has to do with home repair? Even though it's not directly related to your home repair skills, it has a lot to do with succeeding financially using those skills. Getting people to choose you and even pay you more than others in the field is essential to your success. Good communications skills ensure your message will get across to prospects who will become customers.

Never Stop Learning

The second thing is to learn everything you can about home repair. Never assume that you know everything necessary to succeed in your business. It's not enough to know how to repair a few things. Be prepared for bigger jobs as time progresses.

Learn from every job, from every other handyman, from magazines, from the web, and from the completed work of others. Every time you visit anyone's home keep your eyes and your mind open. See how things were done and determine how you might improve on them. Fill your head with new ideas on how to do things.

Go to trade shows and talk with other handymen. Learn what others are doing and how and why they are doing those things. Find out if those methods will work for you. Perhaps they will serve as the basis for some new methods of your own. Don't just accept existing methods as the end all. Create your own ways of doing things.

Think about how to do things better, faster, easier. Learn how to help your potential customers get the exact job they want or need and how to do it the best way possible. You will have to visualize the project and explain everything clearly to your customers.

Visualize and Share Your Vision With Customers

Don't be from the school that believes you are the expert and the customer doesn't merit explanations. Take the time to explain how you would go about it and why one thing works better than others. If you are from that old school of "I'm the expert and I always know the best way to do things," it's time to get over yourself.

Customers prefer to deal with experts who are willing to explain things even if they don't really understand it all. It gives them a feeling that you value their ideas and desires and they would be better off dealing with you, even if it means paying more than the lower bid. Be an expert who helps people to understand your work and they will flock to you and pay your prices without complaint.

Use Drive Time To Learn

You will probably be driving to various locations to bid jobs and to work on the ones that you get. Instead of spending that time listening to news, music, sports or letting your mind chatter away with useless and often negative messages, listen to motivational messages on your Smartphone or CDs. There are many good ones on the market. Earl Nightingale, who died many years ago, had many excellent books and tapes that are now available as audiobooks. His tape set entitled **Lead The Field,** published in 1972, was my favorite. You can probably get a copy from the Conant Company or at some used bookstore. Try a search on Google to find copies of this great tape set.

Such tapes help to instill the values that are important to any one, especially self-employed persons.

Always Go The Extra Mile

Go the extra mile for all your customers. Don't nickel and dime them for small items. Price your work so you don't need to sweat the small stuff. Never make promises that you can't keep. Always deliver what and when you say you will. If a serious problem arises and you can't begin or finish exactly on time, contact your customer as soon as you know about the problem. Don't wait until the last minute and just not show up. Treat all your customers as the most important people in your business because they are.

Be confident and positive with your customers because it builds trust. Never criticize your competition to a potential customer. Sell yourself and your work in a positive manner. If your competitor is doing poor work, his reputation will follow him. Mentioning or dwelling on the poor quality of a competitor's work will give potential customers a negative impression of you and may well cost you a job.

Remember the Golden Rule

Treat customers in the way you would like to be treated. Even though this is simple and the fair thing to do, it's actually quite rare. Most people are simply thinking of their own interest and fail to put themselves in the customer's shoes. If an unpleasant situation arises and you don't know exactly how to respond to it, stop and reflect before you act. This will result in the action that is best for you, your customer, and your business.

Stay Positive

Maintain a positive attitude at all times. Sometimes this is hard to do but it will help you do the best possible job at all times. Know your limitations but be prepared to expand your knowledge to overcome those limitations over time. A positive state of mind will help maintain your health and your business and keep you in that important learning mode. Most people dislike doing business with negative individuals. Fear and doubt can overwhelm almost anyone. Potential customers may sense your doubt and hesitate to contract you for a job.

Remember your love for the freedom of self employment and what a great opportunity it is to make your living doing something you really enjoy. Few people have that unique experience. You can make a good living doing creative and challenging work but don't jump in if you have serious security issues and need a secure income and regular benefits.

Persons with those needs should find a job that offers such security in order to maintain peace of mind. Risk is always a part of self-employment since you no longer have a steady paycheck. Before leaving a regular job to jump into home repair full time, you should enjoy this work enough to accept some risks. If you aren't certain, you can still start on a part time basis until your confidence grows.

Finally, remember that the home repair business is seldom an opportunity to become wealthy. Then again, neither are most jobs, so enjoy your work and good luck.

Covid-19 - The Pandemic

As I write this revised edition, Covid-19 is wreaking havoc with the United States. Some eight million people have contracted it, and some two hundred and fifteen thousand have died from it.

No one knows how long it will be before there is a vaccine. Most of your customers will be concerned about any stranger visiting their home.

Acknowledge that concern by wearing a mask and socially distancing. It may be wise even to wear gloves.

No matter how your customers view the pandemic, you must follow the correct protocol to protect yourself and your customers from possible exposure to Covid. If your potential customer has a problem with this behavior, you should avoid that job.

Special Note From Bill

Some of you already have good home repair skills. Others may be good carpenters who know how to install crown moldings and other fine woodwork. If so, use those skills to gradually expand your business into higher paying work.

Learn from the Internet. Google is an invaluable source of information for almost any business. Take the time to search for the kind of information you need for any job. You will find concise and down-to-earth instructions for most home repair tasks. Remember, use it as a source and then apply your creativity to develop original methods.

Use your handyman experiences to learn more about working with wood in other ways. There are many books on woodworking and the woodworking business that can help you to increase your skills, challenge yourself, and make much more money. As you gain those skills, practice them on projects for your own home to make certain that you can do a good job with them. Then practice more on family and friends until you're confident of your skills.

Positive Imaging, LLC offers two paperback book that may help you to learn the skills needed to expand your business into these areas. The title of the one related solely to the business is "**Woodworking Business: Start Quickly and Operate Successfully.**" I know you will find it a valuable book and you can get complete information about it at: http://woodworking-business.com . You can purchase it from that web site or find it at Amazon.com Books.

The second book is geared to building functional pieces for your home or others. The title is **Woodworking Simplified Book 1: Your How-To Guide For Making Attractive and Functional Projects.** It includes complete instructions and drawings for desks, cabinets, bookcases, tables and more. It's another valuable book that you can find at http://woodworking-simplified.com or at Amazon.com Books.

Disclaimer

Everything described in this book is based on my personal experience. Over the years I've gained considerable experience in construction, home repair, and woodworking and am a competent, though not extraordinary, businessperson. Anyone with good skills may be able to attain similar results if he or she puts in the effort. Nevertheless, no guarantees are expressed or implied regarding your own results using the information in this book.

Some individuals are more apt to profit from home repair than others due to the level of their skills, business acumen, and communication ability. Regardless of my experience over the years, I can't guarantee that you will succeed in this or any business.

Business of any kind involves the risk of loss, including, but not necessarily limited to: money, time, and energy. In addition to the financial and time considerations, home repair involves the use of tools that can inflict serious injuries if used carelessly. I have made every effort to accurately describe my experiences in detail, including safety considerations, but cannot be held liable for any damages or injuries that may result from the use of this information–even if the user informs me prior to or after these damages or injuries occur.

The user of this information agrees that he or she is solely responsible for the consequences of such use. It is also the user's responsibility to conduct a reasonable level of due diligence prior to making any business or legal decisions. The information contained and distributed in this book is not intended as nor should it be considered professional, business, or legal advice.

For any questions please contact bill@positive-imaging.com

Glossary

Accounting: a precise record of the financial transactions of your business.
Accounting Software: software used to maintain information on the financial transactions of your business.
Addendum: An addition to a contract to describe additional work or changes to the existing agreement.
Advertising: The activity of attracting public attention to your products or services.
After Market: similar to third party vendors meaning an accessory or attachment made for a tool or product by another manufacturer.
Analyze: to study how best to perform a certain task to maintain safety and avoid injury.
Backlog: home repair projects under contract and awaiting completion for your customers.
Bank Account: a fund at a bank where you can deposit and withdraw funds.
Belt Sander: a power tool that uses a circular belt with an abrasive grit for sanding surfaces smooth.
Billing: The process of sending an invoice to your customers for services rendered.
Capital: funds available to pay the costs of operating a business.
Carbide Tipped: blades and bits that have carbide attached so they will cut more efficiently and remain sharp longer.
Carpenter: a skilled worker who builds, makes, or repairs wooden objects or structures.
Circular Saw: a power saw for cutting wood consisting of a toothed disk rotating at high speed.

Clamps: metal or wooden instruments used to hold wooden parts together while glue dries.
Collection: obtaining payment for your work.
Communication Skills: the ability to convey your point regarding your work clearly and concisely to facilitate selling home repair projects.
Competent: sufficiently qualified to perform the work required.
Complaints: expressions of dissatisfaction with something.
Compressor: a device that compresses air for use with pneumatic tools.
Consumer Tools: tools that are manufactured to lesser standards because of lighter use by non-professionals.
Contract: an agreement between two of more parties to ensure completion of a project and payment for the work.
Creativity: the ability to be original and to develop new ideas using older ideas as a basis or starting point.
Crown Molding: a decorative molding that is applied at the top of a wall, most often against the ceiling.
Customer: an individual or company that purchases your products or services.
Deposit: advance payment collected to ensure full payment on jobs.
Depreciation: a loss in value due to age or wear.
Drawings: line sketches that clearly describe the construction details for a job or project.
Drill: a power tool for drilling holes in wood or metal.
Employee: a person who works for you in return for financial or other compensation.

Expenses: costs associated with running your business.
Expert: a person with a high degree of skill or knowledge on a particular subject.
Finish Sander: a vibrating power sander used for the final sanding on a job.
General Contractor: a person who is responsible for and supervises the activities of those working on a project.
Gross Income: the total income received from your business activities before expenses are deducted.
Hand Tools: tools for various kinds of work that do not require electrical power.
Health Care: the insurance and facilities required to maintain the health of individuals.
Hourly Rate: the amount per hour paid to yourself or employees.
Income Tax: the tax collected by government from every citizen based on the amount of income they make.
Insurance: a contract by a party indemnifying another against a specified loss.
IRS: Internal Revenue Service collects income taxes.
Lacquer Thinner: a liquid used to clean surfaces of lacquer finishes and to thin lacquer.
Learning: the process of acquiring knowledge about certain skills.
License: an authorization from a government body allowing you to perform some form of business.
Maintenance: keeping tools and buildings in good repair.
Materials: products used to repair, build, or make projects or jobs.

Measurements: the dimensions of a specific project used to cut the parts.
Nails: a pointed piece of metal pounded into wood as a fastener.
Net Income: the income left over after all expenses are deducted from the gross income of a business.
Occupational License: an authorization to participate in a certain occupation or business activity.
Online Banking: conducting your banking using the Internet.

Ordinances: laws that apply to various aspects of your work

activities. **Overhead:** the cost of operating a business.

Paint Thinner: a liquid used to clean or thin oil-based paint.
Payroll: salary paid to individuals for work performed.
Payroll Taxes: taxes deducted from individuals for payment to the IRS.
Penalties: fees charged for not adhering to regulations.
Pneumatic Nailer: a pneumatic tool that drives nails into wood.
Professional: a qualified person engaged in a certain activity for their livelihood.
Profit: what is left after all operating expenses and material costs are deducted from gross income.
Random Orbit Sander: a power sander that rotates and orbits to sand rapidly without creating circular marks on a wood surface.
Reserve Fund: money set aside for one or more specific purposes.
Router: a power tool with a sharp bit used to cut grooves and decorative edges.
Saber Saw: a power saw used to cut curved lines and cutouts in wood.

Safety: steps taken to remain free from danger, risk or injury.
Sanding: the process of smoothing wood in preparation for finishing.

Sanding Belts: circular sanding strips used on belt sanders to sand wood.

Sandpaper: abrasive sheets used to smooth wood surfaces.

Sawhorses: four legged supports to raise work from floor level.
Screws: a metal pin with incised threads used as fasteners. **Security:** the idea or concern about being secure and safe. **Self-Employed:** working for yourself in a business.

Self-disciplined: being able to perform required tasks without having someone to make certain things are done.
Self-motivated: being a self starter who does not require an external motivating force.
Small Business: varying definitions exist but basically it is a business that is not considered large.
Social Security: a fund that individuals pay into in order to have funds available for retirement.
Specifications: details that describe the specifics of a job or project.
Subcontractor: a self-employed individual who works on a project or job for the individual in charge.
Supply and Demand: the process of setting prices on products based on the demand for them.
Trade Tools: tools manufactured for professionals in various fields.
Visualize: to study the steps involved in doing anything before actually performing the tasks.

Wages: hourly fee paid to employees.
Waste Factor: the amount of material that must be calculated in a job because it will be wasted during the cutting.

9.951 845673LV00017B/2449 [430806336]

www.ingramcontent.com/pod-product-compliance
Lightning Source LLC
LaVergne TN
LVHW090133160826
845673LV00017B/2449